Contents

Some words are shown in bold, **like this**. You can find out what they mean by looking in the glossary.

What is a garden habitat?

A garden is an area of land next to a house. Many plants and animals live in gardens.

A place where plants and animals live is called a **habitat**.

Garden habitats provide food and **shelter** for the things that live there.

Animals and plants have special features that help them live in gardens.

What plants grow in gardens?

If you look in a garden, you will find many different types of plants. You might see grass, trees and flowers.

Some people grow fruits and vegetables in their gardens.

Plant leaves take in sunlight to make food for the plant.

Trees grow well in gardens. Their tall trunks lift their leaves up high, so they can catch lots of light.

Weeds grow in gardens too. Weeds are wild plants that people do not want in their gardens.

A stinging nettle is a weed. It has stinging hairs on its leaves and stems to stop animals from eating the plant.

stinging hairs

seed

A dandelion is a weed. Its leaves taste bad to stop animals from eating them.

Dandelions have special **seeds** that catch the wind. They can fly to other places and grow into new plants.

How can plants help animals in gardens?

Garden plants provide food for animals. Animals eat their leaves, fruit and **seeds**.

Plants can provide a home or **shelter** for animals too.

Some insects and birds feed on nectar.
Nectar is a sweet liquid made by many flowers.
Honeybees collect nectar from flowers to
make honey.

How do animals make homes in gardens?

Woodlice live in damp **habitats**. They can be found under rocks and logs in gardens.

A rock or log is a **microhabitat**. A microhabitat is a very small habitat within a larger habitat.

Many birds make nests in gardens. Birds' nests provide warmth and **shelter** for baby birds.

Starlings make nests in holes in buildings and trees. They use their pointed beaks to join bits of grass, leaves and other parts of plants together.

How do animals feed in gardens?

Earthworms eat dead plants and animal waste found in soil. Their poo makes soil better and helps plants to grow.

Earthworms do not have eyes. They spend most of their time underground.

Frogs eat insects, snails, slugs and worms. They live near garden ponds.

Frogs have long, sticky tongues to help them catch **prey**.

Garden spiders eat insects. They live on bushes and plants in gardens.

Garden spiders use **webs** to catch flying insects. Insects get stuck when they fly into the sticky webs.

Squirrels eat nuts and **seeds**. Their large front teeth help them break into hard shells.

In autumn, squirrels store nuts, so they have food for winter.

How do animals protect themselves in gardens?

Ladybirds have bright colours to tell **predators** that they taste bad.

They release a smelly yellow liquid when they feel as if they are in danger.

Garden snails need water to keep them from drying out. They often come out at night or after rain.

Garden snails hide in their shells to protect themselves from drying out in the sun. They come out when it is wet again.

Which garden animals can you see at night?

Foxes mostly come out at night to look for food. They have powerful eyesight, so they can see in the dark.

Foxes also have excellent hearing. Their large, pointy ears can move to pick up sound from all around.

Bats use sound to find their way in the dark.
They call out as they fly.

When the sound hits another object, an **echo**
bounces back. Bats can tell where objects are
by the sound of the echo.

That's amazing!

Long-tailed tits use silk from spiders' egg cocoons to help build their nests. As their chicks grow, the nests stretch to fit them in!

Picture glossary

 **echo** the repeating of a sound as it bounces back off an object

 **habitat** a place where an animal or plant lives

 **microhabitat** a very small habitat within a larger habitat

 **predator** an animal that hunts other animals for food

 **prey** an animal that is hunted by other animals for food

 **seed** a small part of a flowering plant that grows into a new plant

 **shelter** a place that protects from danger or bad weather

 **web** a thin structure made of connecting threads; spiders make webs out of silk thread that they make in their bodies

Find out more

Books

Collinson, Clare. *In the Garden.*
  (Franklin Watts, 2010)

Llewellyn, Claire. *Ways Into Geography.*
  (Franklin Watts, 2012)

Websites

www.bbc.co.uk/nature/collections/p00fxg0m
Watch videos of plants and animals in garden habitats.

www.rspb.org.uk/wildlife/wildlifegarden/animals.aspx
See an A to Z list of wildlife garden species.

Index